MW00626758

Printed in the United States of America.
First Printing, 2021

Publisher

Williams Commerce, LLC

Visit Our Website

Williamscommerce1.com

ISBN: 978-1-736637-7-6

The Number 55

When you think about the meaning
of numbers or angel numbers as
they're often referred to, you quickly
realize that each number has a deeper
meaning behind them. The number
55 is often associated with letting go
of things in your life that no longer
serve a positive purpose. By doing so,
you put yourself in direct alignment
with welcoming new positive
beginnings into your life.

The number 55 resonates with me personally because as I've embarked on new journeys throughout my life, I've realized just how important it is to let go of certain things and people from my past. In order to grow and become everything you're meant to be in this life, it's critical that you learn when to cut ties. Although it's proven to us more and more each day just how short life is, it's imperative that you don't allow yourself to live in the past. Instead, live in the present and make the most out of each

Feeding a voracious mind is

equivalent to saving a drowning

fish!

Losing something that wasn't

worth being kept isn't a loss.

The biggest misconception is

thinking we have time.

Purpose is priceless.

Procrastination is the enemy of

progress.

Maturity comes with knowing

when to accept when something

isn't for you.

Set your own boundaries or

others will set them for you.

Always depend on self, you'll run

out of breath counting on others.

Nothing fools you better than the

lies you tell yourself.

Stop letting your past hold you

prisoner.

Don't spread yourself thin trying

to prove your worth to those

who could never see it.

Memories don't exist without

experiences.

Don't make the same mistakes

today that you made yesterday.

It's ok to seek closure, but never

wait on it though.

No answer is an answer.

Too much pride can stunt your

healing and growth.

Sometimes you don't receive

what you feel you deserve

because it's just simply not your

turn yet.

When the tables turn be prepared

to turn with them.

Everlasting change comes when

the root motivation is self.

The easy days should be the days

you fear the most.

Stop letting others penalize you

for not being perfect.

Whoever you lose in the process

of trying to discover your

purpose in life wasn't meant to be

there.

Stop allowing yourself to fall

victim to comparison.

If you look at respect as being a

one-way street....you're going to

end up at a dead end.

The inability to communicate

effectively will always cause the

demise of any relationship.

Don't value yourself based on

someone else's view of your

worth, they're going to

shortchange you every time.

Common things happening to

uncommon people becomes a

great tragedy.

The greater the distance you are

from yourself, the deeper the

pain reaches.

You must continuously apply

pressure to the coal; the reward

of the diamond should strictly be

viewed as an independent

variable.

Hypocritical actions fueled by

mended hearts could never hold

any merit.

Suicide should also be defined as

continuously doing the things

that we know in our

subconscious and conscious

minds that are going to ultimately

lead to our demise.

The most important component

of any structure is the foundation,

without an unyielding foundation

that structure is most certainly

destined for nothing less of

demolition…annihilation…and

eradication.

Leaps of faith aren't made by

those who are afraid of heights.

The same foot does not lead

every step along the journey;

compromise and balance are

essential.

Inconsistent thoughts often lead

to consistent failures.

Sometimes the big picture doesn't

start to become clearer until you

take a few steps back.

Who's really at fault when you

become a negative influence on

yourself?

Let your actions support your

words. Let your words support

your actions.

Identical struggles rarely yield

identical outcomes.

The tongue that speaketh truths

and only truths; is the most

sacred.

On most occasions they won't

notice that you've been chopping

at the tree until it falls.

They always tend to say you've

changed when your actions are

no longer beneficial to them.

Love, trust, respect, loyalty, are

earned, not owed.

Should we be held solely

responsible for everything that

occurs in our lives?

Life has taught me to plan for my

past.

Fear and hope can either

debilitate or galvanize you.

People will give up on you, but

never give up on yourself.

To know the severity of karma's impact and still not live accordingly is beyond foolish and detrimental to one's own well-being.

Just as we take ownership of our

wins, we must take ownership of

our loses.

Success takes discipline, discipline

takes success.

You can predict the future if you

just take your time.

The way they react when you tell

them your dreams and goals will

determine if they deserve you or

not.

Tell it like it is, not how you

would like others to view it.

Lies are only as powerful as the

people who believe them.

Learn to love yourself on a

consistent basis.

Made in the USA
Las Vegas, NV
08 August 2021

27487389R10036